MOTIVATING STUDENTS TO CHOOSE SUCCESS PROVEN STRATEGIES TO LEND A HELPING HAND IN MOTIVATING STUDENTS

Titles by Susan Fitzell, M.Ed.:

RTI Strategies for Secondary Teachers

Special Needs in the General Classroom, Strategies That Make It Work

Paraprofessionals and Teachers Working Together

Umm Studying? What's That?: Learning Strategies for the Overwhelmed and Confused College and ~ High School Student

Co-teaching and Collaboration in the Classroom

Please Help Me With My Homework! Strategies for Parents and Caregivers

Transforming Anger to Personal Power: An Anger Management Curriculum for Grades 6 through 12

Free the Children: Conflict Education for Strong & Peaceful Minds

Use iPads and Other Cutting-Edge Technology to Strengthen Your Instruction

Memorization and Test Taking Strategies - Professional Development Training Video Set

MOTIVATING STUDENTS TO CHOOSE SUCCESS

Proven Strategies to Lend a Helping Hand in Motivating Students

Cogent Catalyst Publications

ISBN - 978-1-932995-32-9

FOR ACCESS TO YOUR
FREE
COLLECTION OF
SUPPLEMENTARY MATERIALS
AND VIDEOS, GO TO
MOTIVATE.SUSANFITZELL.COM

To contact the author:

Susan Gingras Fitzell
PO Box 6182
Manchester, NH 03108-6182
Phone: 603-625-6087
Email: SFitzell@SusanFitzell.com

Keep up with Susan on the Web!
* Twitter: @susanfitzell
* Twitter: @TheHomeworkGuru
* Facebook.com/SusanFitzellFB
* Facebook.com/TheHomeworkGuru
* Facebook.com/HowToPreventBullying
* LinkedIn: www.linkedin.com/in/susanfitzell
* Pinterest.com/susanfitzell/
* www.scoop.it/u/susan-gingras-fitzell
* YouTube: SusanFitzell

www.CogentCatalyst.com -
Practical strategy books & products that support parents and educators.

To my son,
Ian,
who has taught me
so very much

Introduction

As an educator and a parent, I have often found that lack of motivation is a way that children, or even adults, express their frustration: *I can't do it, so I just won't address it. I don't know how to do it, so I'll hide from it; I'll avoid it.*

How can school and home develop motivation and success for children?

A Mother's Perspective

I have a son who graduated from Clarkson University with a degree in Mechanical Engineering. This is an amazing achievement because he has two significant learning disabilities. He considers himself dyslexic, but, when he was in the fourth grade, we found out that he has a more complicated condition involving his eyes and his vision. He was in the second grade when we found out he has Central Auditory Processing Disorder.

To give you a little snippet of what that is like, he struggles to filter out background noise, and memorization is challenging for him unless what he's learning is tied to meaningful information or previous learning. So, for a young man with two learning challenges, for him to graduate with an Engineering degree is amazing. How did he do it?

He was motivated to overcome his challenges. He never let them be an obstacle in his path. I must admit, his parents never expected anything less. Our requirement: Do your best.

Motivation? There have been times we've had to really work on what that means. It wasn't always smooth sailing.

My daughter didn't have any learning disabilities and she pretty much sailed through school. In her junior year of high school, she hit a wall and we had to start teaching her study strategies. My way of sneakily getting in all those learning techniques was hiring her to be my assistant during my presentations. I offered her a paid job being my program assistant. She would help me set up and break down and be there if I needed her during the day. I did have one requirement that went beyond my need for support. I explained, "You can't leave the room, because if you leave the room once I'm set up and I need you, you won't be there. So you've got to stay." I was gratified, when I would look her way during the day, to see her listening intently to the strategies I was presenting to my teacher audience.

One day, she was in the dining room writing an essay for a scholarship when I suddenly heard this groaning and screaming, "RAAHRR!" I could hear paper crumpling and then hitting the floor. I peeked around the corner and looked at her and said, "What's the matter, honey?" The floor was covered with crumpled paper balls!

"Mom, they don't teach us how to write about *ourselves* in Honors English. They teach us how to do *research* and write *research* papers. This essay has to be about *me*: three things about *me* and why I should get this scholarship. They don't teach us how to write about me and they want it written in first person. All these years I've been taught to write in third person. On top of that, I don't understand the question. *I don't know what to do!*"

> *"Mom, they don't teach us how to write about ourselves in Honors English. They teach us how to do research and write research papers."*

She had worked on it all week. The deadline for her to have it in the mail was the next day. She was about to give it up. So I said, "Honey, how about trying something that I usually use when my students get writer's block? It's really helped them and it might help you."

First of all, I showed her how to cluster an activity, starting with a mind map and then chunking the paper. She said, "Okay, I'll try it; I'll try it."

And then I said, "Before you do that, I want you to color a mandala."

A mandala is an ancient circular design found in many cultures. The purpose behind using the mandala is that when you color from the outside to the center it calms and focuses attention. It's an ancient tool which has been around in different cultures and faiths for centuries.

I said, "Color from the outside in, and as you're coloring, think about your paper. When you get an idea, stop and write it down, then go back to coloring. You color some more, you get an idea, you go back."

Between the two strategies, the clustering activity, which is a combination of mind-mapping and chunking, and the mandala, she had a draft completed within *one hour*. She'd been working on this all week and she finally had a draft! By that evening, she was off and running and had most of it done. I went to bed. She was up a good amount of the night writing that paper.

In the morning, I found a colored mandala and message on my desk. It read, "Mom, have a very safe and pleasant trip!! :) I love you very much,

thank you for your help and mandala in my time of crisis. The mandala is a very good idea, it worked. I love you!!! ~Shivahn."

Fast-forward to her freshman year in college: I was walking down her dorm hallway and all along the walls and on many of the doors, were mandalas! I entered her room and there were more mandalas. I said, "Honey, what's with all the mandalas all along the hall?"

She explained, "Mom, every time somebody comes to me stressed and ready to quit and doesn't want to be at school any more, I give them a mandala and I say, 'Go color!'"I share these experiences with you to provide a parent's perspective.

So often, we teachers ask children to learn the way we teach, the way the curriculum dictates, the way we learn best, and that does not work for all children. We have youth in our classrooms failing in their educational experience or achieving less than their potential, every day. We often blame their lack of intelligence or lack of motivation for their failure to thrive. I contend that the problem is often education's rigidity in teaching methodology, especially at the secondary level. I wish there was a simple solution to the problem. However, the fix is multi-faceted.

Children Are Born Motivated to Learn

I was a high school teacher. I've never taught kindergarten, but I've coached kindergarten teachers and I've sat in the class with 24 or more of these little guys running round. You may think kindergarten teachers have it easy. No. Not in my opinion.

Kindergarteners usually come to school full of energy and motivation. Over the course of a few years, their school experience, if negative, changes their attitude and enthusiasm for learning. If they experience continual failure they, consequently, become unmotivated. Sometimes, they only lose interest in a specific subject. Sometimes, sadly, they simply begin to hate school.

What Motivates Us to Act?

There are a lot of things that motivate us to act, but what is it that *causes* us to act? Why do we do what we do? What is motivation and what impacts it?

Motivation is what we do, why we do it, the reason we do it; it's what causes us to act. It's the instigator. It's the *reason* to do something.

What impacts it? What stops it? What slows it down? What charges it up?

Personal Power

I've thought a lot about this, and not every expert is going to agree with me. However, I feel this really hits the nail on the head through most of my experiences as a parent and as a teacher: Lack of motivation is about personal power. There's also a solid body of research that supports that empowerment (Nichols, 2006) and self-regulation (Cleary & Zimmerman, 2004) are keys to intrinsic motivation.

Think about the youth in class that you can't get to do anything. They won't pick up their head, won't pick up the pencil and won't do anything. Who has the power in that situation? The youth has the power. For some children, that's the only way they can exert their power.

Who has the power to change the youth's behavior? The youth has the power. It's a lot about personal power.

It's about having the resources, the opportunity and the ability to be in control of their destiny. Empowerment always increases the probability that humans will increase effort and motivation (Bénabou & Tirole, 2003).

Let's look at it from this standpoint: If lack of motivation is about personal power, we might hypothesize that the refusal to do school work is an exertion of power. When someone feels they don't have control over their own destiny in life, or any way to exert personal power, they don't act. Choosing not to act is a choice and exercising a choice gives a sense of control (Brooks & Young, 2011).

It works both ways; both sides of the coin impact motivation. If I don't have the resources to be successful, or the opportunity to be in control of my own destiny, I may not have motivation. I may not even be motivated to do anything, because I don't feel like I have any control: *I can't do it, so why should I try? This doesn't mean anything to me* (Gordon, 2006).

The Roles We Play

There are reasons we play conscious and unconscious roles, and each role we play has its

Roles we play: I don't care. It doesn't bother me. I can't do it. I need help.

consequences and effects. For some children it's about whatever role they've chosen.

The 'maps and pictures in our head' and 'rules in our minds about how the world should be' cause us to react to events with unconscious roles. Rather than making a conscious choice to act, we make unconscious choices to 'play the part' we need to play to survive, according to our view of the world. Awareness of these unconscious roles and rules are a critical step to managing our behavior and making conscious choices about how we manage our behavior and emotions. The 'roles we play' may not always allow us to make the choices that best serve our needs over the long term.

Let's take one example: If a student feels like they are incapable of being successful – maybe they're struggling to read, maybe they're struggling to do the math – sometimes they decide that they're not capable, so they play the role of: *I don't care. It doesn't bother me. I can't do it. I need help.*

They play the role to help them get through the situation, avoid the situation, or have an excuse for their failure.

Why are they behaving the way they're behaving? Because it's working for them to

avoid; because it's working for them to demonstrate their power:
For some students, this is the reason they don't try, though there are always exceptions.

Climbing the Cabinets Worked for Him

I had a high school student on my caseload who, when you looked at his appearance, you wouldn't know that he was any different than any other student. He had the social skills to play the role of tough, street-wise punk down pat. He knew how to appear as if he had everything under control and was someone not to be messed with. In reality, his language ability was at a six- or seven-year-old level. Nobody really understood this except those of us who worked closely with him.

He didn't talk like a six year old. He didn't look or act that young. He was a tough-looking teen. It was truly hard for him to function in school and people always thought that he knew more than he did, and was just being bad, or looking for trouble.

One day, he was in Biology and the special education office got a phone call. A panicked teacher exclaimed, "Somebody's got to come get him. Somebody's got to come and get him!" "Why?"

"He's literally climbing the cabinets. Somebody's got to come get him."

When an administrator arrived, my student was on top of the counter in the Biology class leaning against the cabinets that held all the lab equipment and chemicals. He was immediately removed from the class and a team meeting was called to discuss the issue. The team decided he could not return to that class. It simply was not safe for him to be there.

Why did he climb the cabinets? It was the day of a test. Well, it's certainly guaranteed that if you get up out of your seat and climb the cabinets during a test – you get out of the test!

And nobody knows it's because you're really incapable, they just think you're a bad boy. And being a bad boy is cool! That worked for him. I was subsequently assigned to teach an individualized Biology class for this student so he could get his credits for graduation. Once he received an individualized program at his level, he was able to do so much more than we ever thought. When instruction met his needs and was engaging at a level where he could be successful, he did his work. He was motivated!

Sometimes, what people do, they do because of how effective it is. For him, his outrageous behavior was incredibly effective as an avoidance technique.

Our Pervasive Culture of Blame

We live in a culture of blame. You might have noticed that. Everything is everybody else's fault. This is reinforced by television, by media, by what we see in the news. Like the lawsuits resulting in high insurance rates; everything is somebody else's fault.

One of the things that children struggle with is taking ownership for their own behavior. Why is that a problem? Because if you don't believe that you are responsible for your own behavior, then you can't change it.

When We Blame, We Give Away Our Power

If I believe that you did something to me and that made me do something else: *You made me mad; you made me do it;* – then I have given you the power of control (S. G. Fitzell, 2007).

If you have the power of control, then I don't have it, and if I don't have it, then I can't be motivated. Why would I be motivated? I don't have a choice. I can't do anything, because you have the control; it's your fault.

Not every youth exhibits this belief system, however, it's a concerning issue in our society.

Even I have had to come to grips with this. I grew up in a generation where I learned and repeated: *You made me mad!*

Well, if you made me mad, then you're the one that has to change, not me! It's about you, it's not about me. You made me fail (Ellis, 1999).

This is another piece we want to look at: How do you take ownership? Because when we blame, we give away our power (S. G. Fitzell, 2007).

If motivation is about personal power, then the personal power we have affects and impacts our motivation. When we own our behavior and we say, *"Okay, I own it. I own my reaction. I own what I do about it. I own how I take charge. I own it."* Then we can do something about it. If we can do something about it, then we might be more motivated to act.

Nurture Ownership

I used to use this analogy with my students. I co-taught an anger management program for five-and-a-half years. Four-and-a-half years were at the high school in Londonderry, New Hampshire, where I was teaching, and, one year was at a middle school in Manchester, NH. We ran three 8-week sessions for 8-12 students per year.

It's really challenging to get the concept of ownership across to youth: The teacher didn't make you mad. He may have triggered your anger; she may have 'pushed your buttons.' However, the teacher didn't *make* you mad. How you reacted was a choice, even though it might have triggered your anger.

When you say someone's made you mad, it's like you're a puppet on a string

When these children feel like they have no control, I say to them, "When you don't take control of your own behavior, when you say someone's made you mad, it's like you're a puppet on a string and you're letting somebody else control the string. Because if I say, 'You made me mad,' who has the power? The other person does.

"But if I say, 'You *triggered* my anger.' Who has the power? I do."

It's just linguistics; it's just the way we phrase it. Think about it. We want children to own it.

When students would accuse me of making them mad, I replied consistently, "No, I didn't make you mad. I may have triggered your anger, I may have pushed your buttons, but you're the one in control of you."

Ownership: If I own it, then I feel I have control. I have personal power. If I have personal power, I'm going to be more motivated.

Learned Helplessness

Learned helplessness can sometimes be a result of our doing too much for children when we're trying to help them. It's a common problem when working with students with special needs; adults struggle to know how much help is too much. Learned helplessness is a concept that is considered to be a cognitive process where students perceive events which are controllable to be out of their control, and perhaps at times will see uncontrollable events as controllable (Peterson, Maier, & Seligman, 1993).
There have been research studies done to determine the effect of a paraprofessional–student relationship on student achievement and

success. These studies concluded that a significant number of children who had paraprofessional support experienced learned helplessness. The cause was determined to be related to how much is done for students by well-intentioned paraprofessionals. Sometimes parents require schools to provide support that may hinder the paraprofessional from providing students with opportunities to develop independence.

When youth depend on a paraprofessional to be successful in school, the youth then begins to feel like they're not in charge of themselves. They lose their sense of personal power: *I don't have any power; I can't do that. I need help* becomes their mantra.

Helping students who have learned helplessness to become confident, independent and motivated to work on their own requires specific verbal scripts so as not to further solidify the students' sense of helplessness. The research says that if you try and help a student with learned helplessness and you do it wrong, you very well could make it worse, with all good intention. You really have to know how to talk to children with Learned Helplessness (Miller & Seligman, 1975).

Our Bodies Speak Louder than Our Words

Body Language

Body language is such a big issue and can be discussed from several different angles. I'd like to mention a few scenarios where body language is a powerful tool and correlate how it relates to motivation.

When considering youth and their level of motivation, it's important to understand that their belief about their power to affect their world is impacted by the influential people in their lives. Consequently, we must ask ourselves: What is our body language telling our children about their worth, their potential, and their esteem? The messages we send do not only come from the words we speak. Words are a small part of the equation. Our tone and body language speak the loudest. We must be self-aware and choose our responses carefully (Simon, 1995).

I have been challenged with that in my life. My son, for instance, reads people extraordinarily well. I might say one thing, but he'll know. "No, I know Mom, you're upset," even if I try not to act upset, he can tell.

As a parent, a teacher, or a youth: If I point at someone, is that aggressive, neutral, or assertive? Most consider it aggressive.

Parents: If we're the adult in the situation, and we're frustrated with a child who's not doing what they're supposed to do and, consequently, we shout while pointing at the child, "Take out that paper and get that work done!" we are being aggressive.

Will that show of aggressiveness in tone and body language motivate the child? If that youth is exercising their personal power, they will dig in their heels, which is what my son would do in that situation. My daughter would just tell me what she thought of my behavior – politely.

Think about that. How do we respond to children? There have been times when I look back at my behavior as a teacher and realize that my reaction to a behavior issue in the classroom probably shut the youth down.

It's also important to teach youth how they come across to others via body language and tone of voice.

Is Our Body Communicating Strength or Weakness?

I've taught Martial Arts to youth aged 6-14 for over 20 years. In addition to physical martial arts, I teach bully prevention and mental self-defense. Teaching body language is part of the curriculum and an opportunity to develop self-awareness. If I see children shuffling their feet in my Martial Arts class, I'll use this as a teachable moment. I'll shuffle my feet and say, "Do I look strong or do I look weak?"

"Weak," they always reply. Then, I engage them in a discussion about how to look strong, confident and, therefore, less likely to be a target of bullying.

Then I show them assertive body language. "Now, do I look strong or do I look weak?"

"Strong." They can easily identify the message.

Strong or weak? Assertive or aggressive? Be aware of what this tells others about you.

I explain to the children, "People who are looking for victims are looking for certain body language that is typical of an easy target." Teaching youth about body language is important because their image of themselves impacts their sense of empowerment and, therefore, their motivation.

If children are not doing what I want them to do; if I *get in their face,* will that aggression really motivate them to do what they are supposed to do? Probably not. Some may go through the motions in the moment out of fear, however, long term; they will more likely learn to passive-aggressively rebel or outwardly act out.

Body Language Activity: Aggressive, Neutral or Assertive?

Whether we're a parent, a teacher, or a student, our body language sends a message to those we interact with and those who observe us. Some body language is aggressive and some is assertive; body language may send a negative message, a neutral message, or a positive message. Consider the following list of body language behaviors.

Which behaviors are aggressive? Which are neutral? Which are assertive? Which show weakness?

- Finger pointing
- Shuffling from foot to foot
- Wringing of hands
- Blushing
- Nose-to-nose
- Hands at sides
- Hands on hips
- Nervous cough
- Looking in the eyes
- Looking down and around
- Straightening clothes
- Arms crossed across chest
- Slumped shoulders
-

Body Language from a Different Angle: Look Busy!

Back in the day, where I grew up in Holyoke, Massachusetts, paper mills thrived. I worked on the factory floor during school breaks to pay my way through college. If you are from the United States, it's very possible that when you were young, you carried a notebook binder to school made at National Blank Book Co. Or possibly, you collected your photographs in a photo album from Springfield Photo Mount. It was in those factories that I learned some valuable workplace lessons.

Full-time employees at the mills referred to us college kids as 'little whippersnappers.' I'm pretty certain that was not the only thing they called us.

Employees were either paid by the hour or by the piece. The goal was to work fast and make the quota set by management. If you were paid by the piece, you had to get so many pieces done in an hour and would get a bonus if you went over the goal per hour.

As college students doing this work part-time in the summer, we were not tired or worn out. We knew we would not be doing this work for the rest of our lives. Our goal was to quickly make the quota so we could socialize afterwards! Well, those ladies who were on the line and had been there for twenty-plus years straightened us out, really fast.

They said, "You don't do that!"

"Why?"

"They'll increase the rate. If they figure you can get it done in this short amount of time, they'll want all of us to do that and they'll make it harder for us to make the rate. We're not young anymore like you whippersnappers are. Look busy! Look busy!"

They told us, "No matter what, even if your job is done, when the foreman comes around - look busy!"

So I learned at a young age, no boss wants to see their employees goofing around.

When I'm coaching co-teachers and one of them is in the back of the room providing a support role in the classroom, I often say, "Get a clipboard and collect data. Look busy." Otherwise, an observer might get the impression that the second teacher in the room is not working to capacity.

Look Motivated!

In my coaching work, I've met teachers who literally take on the challenge of teaching students how to look motivated in the classroom, even if they have no interest in the subject. They teach students how body language sends a message to the teacher. If they sit in a position that conveys interest, teachers respond positively to them. They role play various ways to sit and discuss the messages their body language is sending. Interested body language sits up and leans forward with eyes focused on the teacher. The youth are encouraged to try looking interested as an experiment in human behavior.

Looking interested became a game or experiment for the students.

You might think it's inappropriate to teach students to fake out the teacher, however, when students see the positive effect of 'looking motivated' they often continue the behavior and actually become motivated.

How youth comes across also affects how they're perceived, and how they're perceived affects their motivation.

So tell youth, "Okay, even if your mind is elsewhere, if you lean forward and you *look interested,* the teacher will *think* you're interested. If the teacher *thinks* you're interested, you might make that grade. The teacher might even like you better." It works.

Changing Negative Mindsets

The Bully in Your Brain

One summer, between elementary school and middle school, I discovered that a stranger had taken over my son's creative, positive personality. I saw the symptoms of Obsessive-Compulsive Disorder (OCD) overtake my child. It was one of the most painful periods of my life as a parent. He was a different child. I didn't know him anymore. I made an appointment with a psychologist which took weeks to schedule and in the meanwhile, searched for ways to help him deal with his OCD nightmare.

I came across a book titled *Freeing Your Child from Obsessive-Compulsive Disorder* by Tamar E. Chansky, Ph.D. It is, by far, the most practical, common sense, solution book written in lay person's language on the topic of OCD. The author uses analogies, both verbal and visual, to help the reader understand how to approach the issue successfully. For example, one analogy compares OCD thoughts to junk mail.

My take-away from this book was not only relevant to people with OCD. It was relevant to everything we think and believe that feeds the thoughts in our brain. When youth appear to be unmotivated, ask them what they are thinking.

You might get responses similar to these: "Well, they're telling me ... People don't like me," and "The teacher doesn't like me," or "I'm stupid," or "I'm not smart," or "I'm ugly."

A possible way to respond: "Okay, you know what? Those thoughts are like bullies. They are putting you down, telling you bad things about yourself. They are bullying thoughts. I want you to think about the bully in your brain, and you tell that bully that you don't want to listen to him anymore. You are in control of your thoughts."

It felt strange to consider using a strategy such as this with my students, because I feared there might be children who may think they're schizophrenic, or have multiple personalities, if I suggested such a thing. But on the other hand, I knew this really could work!

To my son, I'd say, "There's a bully in your brain. When that bully says those negative things to you, you tell that bully: 'STOP. I'm not listening to you.' And you talk back to that bully in your brain."

When we finally had our first appointment with the psychologist, my son wasn't in the room for fifteen minutes before the doctor came out and told my husband and me that he could not help my son. Stunned, we asked why not. He said, "Your son is refusing my help. He won't talk to me, and told me that he didn't need my help. He said his mom could help him. When I challenged that statement, he argued, 'My mom knows how to help me! She has a book!'"

My husband and I had never seen this side of our son. He's usually very easygoing, talkative, and friendly. He's rarely defiant. My son, however, truly felt that he did not need the psychologist. He was using the techniques I taught him from the book.

On a side note: The psychologist also suggested we have him checked for Pediatric Autoimmune Neuropsychiatric Disorders Associated with Streptococcal Infections (PANDAS). Our paperwork indicated that he had had a severe cold and sore throat in early June and he felt it was possible the culprit was strep. The doctor was right. After a course of antibiotics, my son's OCD disappeared. I took what I learned from my experience with my son to my classroom.

Be a Mind Detective

I was teaching high school at that time and working with struggling learners. Many of my students were 'unmotivated,' felt defeated, believed they were stupid, etc., etc. So, I tried the technique with some students, but instead of saying, "The bully in your brain." I said, "Be a mind detective. You've got thoughts going through your head. As a detective, determine: Are those thoughts negative? Are they positive? Are they telling you good things about yourself or bad things about yourself? What are they telling you? If they're telling you bad things about yourself, tell them to stop it. You are the one in control of your thoughts. You're the detective. When the detective tells you, 'They're saying these bad things,' you tell those thoughts 'No! No more.' Instead, choose thinking that is positive, that helps you to feel smart and powerful."

Use positive self-talk. Positive thinking is significantly related to youth's engagement, self-confidence, imagination, and optimism in the learning process (Hong, Lin, & Lawrenz, 2012).

It sounds a little crazy, but again, it works! It's not all that different from visualizing success. You're changing your thinking. You think it; you feel it; you do it. I've done a lot of research on this type of reprogramming our thoughts, gaining much from the works of Dr. Albert Ellis (Ellis, 2007).

Not everybody subscribes to that psychology, but I do because it works. There's a significant body of research behind it as well as hundreds of years of spiritual teaching out of the Eastern Philosophies. I realize that it is controversial in some religious circles and respect people's right to differ. I, however, cannot remain silent on something that has yielded concrete, positive results and thus freed people from emotional pain.

Fake It Till You Make It

If you're miserable, smile.

Right now, you are reading this book. Chances are you are not smiling in the middle of serious reading. Try smiling. Seriously. Stop reading for a second and smile.

You may feel like you're being really silly, however, you can't smile without actually *smiling*! Try smiling at people that you don't really like. Watch what happens. It's an effective people-skills strategy. People often smile back.

I had a life-changing experience in college when I acted on some advice from one of my dorm mothers. My perception was that I had no friends. Nobody liked me. I thought I was ugly. I hated myself. I had had some dealings with bullying when I was in middle school and high school and it seriously impacted my self-esteem and my self-image.

In my freshman year at college, I got close to my dorm mother, Sister Jeanne. One day, I was telling her how I felt and she said, "You know what, Susan? Why don't you fake it till you make it? Try this experiment: Next time you go into the cafeteria, instead of sitting with the friends that you are comfortable sitting with, try going to a different table where you don't know anybody."

My stomach wrenched just hearing those words. "Are you serious? You want me to sit with people that I don't even *know*?"

She said, "Try it. Just go, sit and listen."

I really loved this sister and I thought: *Okay, I will.* Next time I talked to her, I didn't want her to ask me, "Did you try it?" and have to say, "No."

So, the next day, I went to the cafeteria and sat at a table with people I didn't know. Honestly, I was scared to death. I hid my fear and just smiled, and listened, and smiled some more. And then an amazing thing happened: they asked me questions! They engaged me in conversation and it was eye opening! They didn't say, "Get out."

They didn't ignore me. They didn't say horrible things to me. They were sincerely friendly, and they invited me back the next day. Wow! I was faking it. I didn't feel comfortable at that table. I didn't feel like smiling, I was scared to death! But

I faked it till I made it. After my first successful attempt, I continued the experiment.

Once I had tried and was successful several times with different groups of students, I realized: *Oh, wow! I'm more comfortable. I have more friends. Imagine that! I have more friends!* What changed? Their behavior didn't change. I changed my behavior and they simply responded. It was the first time in my life that I realized that I had the power to create my future.

Sometimes, just carrying yourself in a way that conveys confidence, positivity and motivation, whether you feel that way or not, could be life changing.

Learn How You Learn and Find the Road to Success

Get your power back. Yes, maybe the teacher gave a hard test. *Maybe* you didn't study, or didn't study enough. Or, maybe we need to think about how *we* learn, and not always try to do things the way somebody else says we should do them. Maybe we do our homework, but maybe we also do a little extra the way we like to do it.

That's a hard-sell for some children. My son used to say, "My teacher says write it out three times in cursive, so that's what I have to do," even though he didn't learn that way.

Why should he write it out three times in cursive and fail the test every week? By the fifth week, do you think my son was motivated to write it out three times in cursive? Do you think homework was something he looked forward to? No, not spelling or vocabulary homework. Was it helping him? No!

So, I came up with a compromise.
"Okay, how about you write it two times in cursive, just as the teacher wants, and I'll negotiate with your teacher to allow you to draw the word the third time." So, the third time, we printed the word on a flashcard, added a picture that represented the word and color-coded the word. We practiced five cards a day for the week before the test, just five of them at a time.

Every single time he made flashcards, color-coded with a visual image, and practiced a little bit every day, he aced the test. Finally, I stopped getting involved because he was doing it on his own.

And then one week I saw an 'F' on his test. I asked, "Honey, what happened?"

"I don't know."

"Did you do your flashcards?"

"No."

"Why not?"

"Well, I was doing so good. I thought it was easy, I didn't think I needed to do it anymore."

Every single time he chose not to use the strategy, he failed the test. Eventually, he figured out that he needed to honor the way *he* learned.

My son was one of those children who didn't want any strategies that were different from what the teachers required and the other children were doing. In college, he still didn't want to stand out as a different learner; however, he knew that to succeed, he'd have to sort out a way to use his strategies discreetly. He knows how he learns, and he uses it sometimes, but he won't tell anyone he's using a different strategy. That's fine.

"I don't learn from the teacher," he says, "I go to class and I sit there to *look good*. I'm just in the chair so they count me when they take attendance, then, after class I get together with other kids in my class, or with the teacher's assistant and that's when I learn."

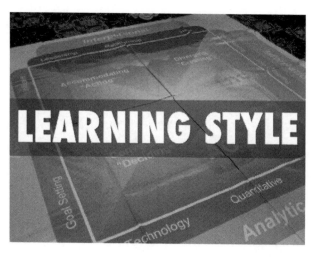

Choose how you learn. Learn how you learn, and choose to learn how you learn! So many children know how they learn and won't do it because they don't want to look different.

In high school Honors classes he didn't learn much from his teachers. He will tell you that straight out, because they all lectured, except for his Chemistry class. That lady let them blow things up – he loved that Chemistry teacher! So, how did he succeed in Honors and Advanced Placement classes? He went to a local coffee shop with his friends, or to somebody's house, and they taught each other.

My son learns best by peer tutoring, watching tutorial videos, and hands-on experiences. My daughter uses a variety of visual study strategies and loves to teach her friends as well. She would broadcast what she was doing to succeed, my son is private; they're different children.

School, Failure and Motivation

Are You Supporting or Enabling?

I was teaching a high school freshman one year who came into class announcing she could not write. I don't mean compose a paragraph. I mean she could not pick up a writing utensil and write.

I read her Individual Education Plan (IEP), and it said she should have a scribe, but it didn't say she *wasn't allowed* to write by herself. So, I was helping her with an assignment. Once she gave the answer, I asked, "Can you write that?" She didn't refuse, yet she hesitated.

I proceeded to encourage her and help her write the answer by herself. She had no problem writing the answer. She worked slowly and needed a little prompting, but she was successful and appeared pleased with her accomplishment.

The next day, her mother called my supervisor and complained that I made her child write. She was furious that I didn't scribe for her daughter. She said, "She shouldn't have to write. It's in her IEP." She demanded that her daughter be removed from my class.

She not only got taken out of my class, but another case manager who took her onto her caseload had to call the mother every week and give a report as to how her daughter was doing and whether her IEP was being followed.

Senior year, her case manager confided in me that the young woman's mom was not looking forward to her daughter's graduation from high school. She said, "Mom's extremely nervous for her daughter."

"Why?" I asked.

"She's got no writing skills. Honestly, she has few life skills. Her mom as coddled her so much all these years, now that she's about to enter the adult world, she's not prepared."

Now, one might claim that's a bad mother. I disagree. That's not a bad mother, that's a mother who doesn't understand that in her attempt to protect her child, she was instilling in her child a learned helplessness. That's a mother who's trying to do the best for her child and who's been so scared her child will fail, that she never allowed her daughter to gain confidence and independence.

Sometimes help is required, sometimes it's not, and sometimes you really have to think about which is which.

As a teacher, there are times when I've had to question: How far do I push? Am I pushing too hard? Am I pushing too little? As a mother, I faced the same issues with my son. How far do I push him? Am I helping too much? Am I helping enough? Luckily he's always been amazing at pushing himself.

He had goals, was motivated to succeed and chose those courses himself; sometimes ignoring my advice to choose what I felt was a more appropriate course load.

Over the years, some of his teachers accused me of pushing him. They looked at his disability and believed that he would not be so successful in school if I was not pushing him. No, I was not pushing him to take those courses.

One of his middle-school teachers warned me that if my son continued to overachieve he was going to end up in a mental institution. He went on to tell me a story of a friend who attempted suicide because he could not meet his parents' expectations. He worried that would happen to my son if I kept pushing him so hard. The truth was, I wasn't pushing my son and my son was much more capable than his teachers gave him credit for.

My son's story had a happy ending. He graduated from college with a degree in Mechanical Engineering. He may not have been at the top of his class. He will always need a proofreader and spellchecker. And, hopefully, he'll be able to afford a house cleaner when he's on his own. For now, he's healthy, successful and thriving.

Never give up on your child and NEVER take someone else's prediction of your child's ability as carved in stone.

Believe in your child, teach your child how to learn, and keep the bar high.

When children focus on what they are good at, they will be motivated to succeed in their area of strength.

The Correct Way to Help a Student

So, how do we help our youth without doing too much for them?

For example: You've got a student who's taking a test and is stuck on a question.

Tell Them What They've Done Correctly

Find something right about what they've done. They don't need to hear what they did wrong. Instead, tell them what they did correctly, so that they feel a measure of personal power and capability.

This strategy is an excellent communication strategy when dealing with anybody, whether in the workplace, in your family, or at school. My personality style is: one who critiques first and my business manager is: one who appreciates first, so if I critique first, he often perceives my critique as hurtful. I've had 14 years of working with him to learn how to appreciate first.

I've had to learn this same approach when communicating with my son. He's the only 'feeling' type personality in my house, and is quite sensitive. Certain personalities really need you to appreciate first, to find out what's right first, and not to go right to the critique. It may seem like it's more efficient to go directly to the point, however, it can be the worst thing you can do and a strong de-motivator.

If it's your personality style to critique first, train yourself to appreciate first. Practice the skill, it will pay off immensely.

Teach the Next Step and Leave!

After you've told them what they've done right, then tell them the next step. Don't get into long explanations; just tell them the next step: *The next step is this.* It may be counter-intuitive. It may seem illogical to not tell them why. But a contributor to learned helplessness is that learning becomes overwhelming (Mikulincer, 1995).

If they're getting it wrong and they're frustrated, and we try to take the time to go through this long explanation about why it's wrong, what to do next and how to do it, that youth is on sensory overload.

Tell them the NEXT STEP

The conversation might sound like this: "Yes, you got that right. You got the notes down just beautifully, there. Here's what you do next. Okay. You're on your own."

Walk Away – Leave and Don't Look Back!

This is the hardest thing to do!

Now, they might say, "But... but can you...?"

No! They may try to guilt you into not leaving them, but no; you go! You walk away. Resist the urge to take care of them! Resist the urge to do it for them! Resist the urge to give in! Resist.

Turn and LEAVE

What I've learned teaching Martial Arts is this:
Sometimes you've got to show them a little and walk away!

Personally, I can relate to this. I realize I learn the same way. If I'm stuck, don't give me a detailed explanation. Just tell me what to do to get to the next step. In that moment of 'stuckness' that's what I need. Teach me the explanation later when there's more time, I'm less frustrated and I'm calm. Or, let me learn on my own in my own time. If you try to give me a long, detailed explanation I'll quickly reach overload. I'm a visual learner, so telling me isn't going to help anyway. Draw me a picture.

Mimicking vs. Being Forced to Think

I have about a dozen children in my Martial Arts class. When teaching them their martial arts forms, we do a continuous series of moves. I stand in front of them and do the forms while they follow along behind me. When they stand behind me and just do beautifully!

Originally, I thought, "These kids are good!" When I first started teaching Kung Fu, I couldn't understand how we could do the same moves for weeks with students following along perfectly, then on a review day, I'd say, "Okay, Johnny, step up to the front and show me '8 Chain Punch.'" and, he couldn't do it.

At some point I realized that my students had simply been copying me! Children are excellent mimics. While we were in class, they had been watching me and copying the moves. Then they went home and couldn't remember the moves to practice on their own.

In looking for a solution, I reflected on how my martial arts instructors taught me. As a new martial arts student, I was frustrated at the expectation that I could be shown a move and two minutes later be expected to practice it on my own. I know what happens in my brain – I forget and have to dig deep to recall what I was shown.

The reality is that in order to internalize new material, you have to make yourself think about what you are supposed to do. You might get it wrong, but at least you're getting your brain and those neural connections working, and that gets it into your memory, a little bit at a time.

If we help youth through the whole process, they won't know how to do it on their own afterwards. It's really hard as a parent or teacher, especially when working with a student who struggles, to walk away and let them sort the learning out. But we must let them practice, so that they learn and remember.

What's the Brain Got To Do With It?

Positive Learning Chemicals vs. Flight or Fight

How does thinking positively help you to learn? It actually releases chemicals in your brain that support learning. It releases dopamine and epinephrine in the right amounts.

I used to think positive thinking was 'fluff'. I'm not a touchy-feely kind of person, so I pooh-poohed it. But the research shows that, biologically, positive thinking literally builds neural connections in your brain. You're actually firing off neurons and dendrites that are releasing dopamine (Shohamy & Adcock, 2010), noradrenalin and other brain chemicals which, in fact, support successful learning.

Negative self-talk releases too much cortisol, which is a stress hormone. Increased levels of cortisol impair working memory (Oei, Everaerd, Elzinga, van Well, & Bermond, 2006). This is not psychological. It's biological.

If I'm stressed, I'm releasing cortisol. Cortisol is your fight-or-flight chemical (Jansen, Nguyen, Karpitskiy, Mettenleiter, & Loewy, 1995) and it's there to protect you from that raging tiger that's coming towards you. Your students and your children don't know the difference between a raging tiger coming towards them and a piece of paper that's a test.

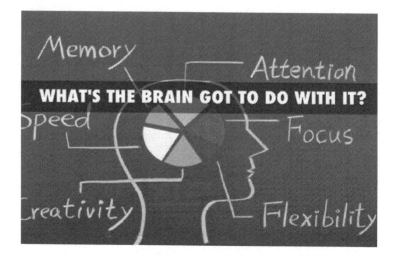

The calmer I am going into a test, the calmer I am going into a learning situation, the better off I am and the more likely that brain chemicals are working in my favor, rather than against me by causing short-term memory impairment.

So, if you're working at home with your child on homework, the minute he gets stressed or upset, he is shut down from learning for about half an hour. It takes about half an hour to come down from a cortisol 'shot.'

Because of the cortisol effect, if homework or schoolwork become so frustrating emotions my escalate, you might as well take a break. Come back to it later. At home, dance, do something fun, laugh, put on a funny 15-minute comedy clip; do something to release the stress and get the positive chemicals going.

At school, do a Brain Gym hook up, or, color a mandala to regain calm and focus before continuing.

Choices Foster Empowered Thinking

As a teacher, teaching for over 30 years in the United States, the one thing that has clearly changed is a move from teaching methods that encouraged cooperative learning, individualized instruction, projects and constructivism, to more whole-class instruction focused on increasing standardized test scores. When I grew up in the '70s, children had a lot more choices in the classroom. We had learning centers and learning centers presented tasks with choices. We had different individualized instruction options in the classroom. We had classes with contracts for grades. We had project options – pick one of the ten suggestions. These learning options provided youth with choices.

I remember when I was in high school in the 70s, any class I was in had a list of ten options for assigned projects, and we could choose which ones we wanted to do. I had one class where I was given a choice of opting for an 'A' a 'B' or a 'C.' The option I chose determined my workload and challenge level for the class. These were classes of 25-30 students with one teacher.

Maybe it's just the schools I've been working with for the past 10+ years, but I don't see that anymore. I see scripted programs. I see: *This is what you've got to do; this is how you've got to do it; this is when you've got to do it.*

Can our students and schools make the grade, but still offer students some choices? No matter how strict your school-district mandates are, we must ask: Are there choices we can offer? Because choices empower, motivate, and foster critical thinking (Brooks & Young, 2011; Flowerday & Schraw, 2000; Simmons & Page, 2010).

Think about it. How many of us, as adults, like it when someone says to us, "I need you to do such-and-such. I need it by Friday. And by the way, you have to do it exactly my way."

Imagine the conversation goes like this:

You: "Oh, but, you know what? I know another way..."

Boss: "NO! I'm sorry. This is the way it has to be done."

You: "But... but I think... You know, we could save some time and be more efficient, and actually might engage more..."
Boss: "You just do your work."

Imagine your boss saying to you, "You've got to do it this way, by this time. You have absolutely no choice."

How would you like working for that boss? Maybe you do work for that boss. Is it a motivating environment to work in?

On occasion, people will say, "Well, sometimes, I just like to know what I have to do so I don't have to think. I just do it. I feel more secure when I know exactly what to do. "

Sometimes that works for us, but would we want that with absolutely everything? That's what's happening to our children in many of our classrooms. The downside is that our children are not getting practice at making choices, learning from those choices, and taking ownership of their learning.

Offering Choices:

- May reduce or prevent problem behaviors
- Can offer independence
- Can increase motivation and productivity
- Can prevent learned helplessness
- Can increase attention to task (Kohn, 1993)

Scripts for Offering Choice

Choose Any Ten Questions or Problems on a Given Page

A typical math assignment is to do the odd-numbered problems on a page of the math text. Of course, students immediately start at number one. If they get it wrong or they struggle with it, they're supposed to go to number three, right?

So they try number three, and they get it wrong again. They're more frustrated; maybe they don't know what to do. Maybe the negative thinking in their brain is telling them they can't do math, or that they are stupid.

So, if they could not do number three, what's the chance that they're going to attempt number five? Very slim.

What if, instead of saying, "Do the odd numbers," we say, "You can do any ten questions or problems on page..."

Encourage students to pick the easy ones first to start the assignment. What's the youth going to do? They're going to look down the page and they're going to look for one that they can do – the easy one. They're going to do that one and hopefully think, "Number seven is easy. I can do seven. Okay."

Chances are that they'll try another one if they felt successful with number seven.

Offering choices can make a difference. It won't make a difference with 100% of the students, but it will make a difference for most students (Bluestein, 2008; S. Fitzell, 2010).

Do the Assignment in Any Order You Choose

When writing an essay, why do we have to start with the introductory sentence? Possibly, you've always wanted to write a novel, so you take a writer's workshop. The first thing the instructor is going to tell you to do is to "just start writing."

You don't have to start at the beginning. Start anywhere. Just start! I've written several books. Only one draft started at the beginning, because in that book, the first chapter introduces the framework and foundation for the whole book. With that chapter, I submitted a random chapter. I did not submit chapters one and two. To submit the proposal to the publishing company I had to give them two sample chapters. Did I actually start on page one? No.

Linear thinkers may prefer to start writing by creating a linear outline and following it in order. Random thinkers will work better with a mind map of the points to be covered, an accordion file to hold their physical research, online organizers and loose paper, or a mobile note-taker to write their thoughts down in chunks.

For more information about Clustering, a writing strategy, get Shivahn Fitzell's book, Umm... Studying? What's That? at www.amazon.com

Choose Three of the Ten Activities Listed

What about, instead of saying, "You have to do X," give them two or three choices out of ten tasks. Sometimes ten choices might be too many. Whether two out of five, or one out of three, the key is that it is important to give students choices. Students are more motivated when they can choose because, again, they are exercising their personal power to choose for themselves. They have more buy-in to the task.

Choose Where to Sit (Or Stand) for Independent Activities

Why do students have to sit at a desk? Some students will spend all of their time, whether consciously or unconsciously, looking for ways to get away from their desk.

We often assign specific seats to students to control class behavior and maintain focus and attention. However, would it be reasonable to allow students to choose where to sit during specific activities? What if we required students to sit in assigned seats for direct teaching, yet allowed them to sit where they want for independent work?

Even in high school, students might prefer to sit on the floor to work or collaborate. Why not allow them to sit where their bodies are more comfortable? Class rules still need to be reiterated and enforced. If they sit with their friend and they're off-task, then they may need an adult to make the choice of where to sit for them. Be certain that they understand this would be a logical consequence of their choice.

What if they ask to stand? I had students who struggled to sit in the classroom and I realized one day that if I allowed them to stand and work off the bookcase, they were more focused and their behavior significantly improved. When my son was little, he'd eat better if he could stand at the dining room table. It also minimized trips to the hospital after he fell out of his chair.

And as for myself, I can't sit to focus. I actually create a standing station in my office with a lap desk on top of the desk, and in a hotel room by placing an upside-down drawer on the desk. I put my laptop on top of the drawer.

Why do we have to sit in a certain place all class period? Or even at home for our homework? There are 'How To' homework help books that'll advise parents to set up a quiet spot for the youth to have a place to do their work. That works for some children, but for some children we need to change that paradigm a little bit. Help students find out how and where they learn best and encourage them to use what they know about their learning style to succeed.

You May Have a One-Minute Break Now, or a Three-Minute Break Later

You're working with a student who doesn't want to work; he's unmotivated. You are hearing a litany of excuses: *I'm tired. I don't want to work. I don't want to do this. My hand hurts, etc.* Say, "Okay, I understand you are tired. How about if I give you a one-minute break now, and then you can do the work after the timer rings. Or I could give you a three-minute break a little later. One minute now or three minutes later; what do you choose?"

Set Parameters

When my daughter was two, I was reading all the books on how to raise a child. I made a conscious choice to raise my children from an informed point of view.

I read that it was important for children to have opportunities to make choices. What choices can you give a two year old? That's easy, I decided: She can pick out her clothes. So, I allowed her to choose her own outfits.

One day she picked up this combination of clothes that was horrid. I thought I was supposed to be a good mother and honor her choices. However, that day's outfit was quite embarrassing. I brought her to her home daycare and I said to the woman who was caring for my child, "I'm trying to be a good mother and let her pick out her clothes." I explained, "Really, I didn't pick that."

Why do students have to sit at a desk? Some students will spend all of their time, whether consciously or un-consciously, looking for ways to get away from their desk.

She laughed. When I came to pick my child up that night she said, "Here's what you do. The night before, after you put her to bed, pick out two outfits. Leave them out. The next morning when she gets up, tell her 'Here are your two choices. Pick one of these two.' Don't just let her pick anything she wants."

I worried that my daughter would balk at just two choices. Well, she didn't. Mornings were much smoother after that.

> *One of the most helpful things a parent can do is allow children to accept responsibility for their consequences and their actions.*

Guiding Strategies & Consequences

Once children get past the first grade stage of wanting to please the teacher – *I want to do this because the teacher will like me; I want to please the teacher* – motivating youth to do what the teacher tells them becomes more challenging.

Relationship does come into play when children are older, so there are some secondary-school students who will do things to please the teacher, however, for the most part, they have moved beyond that impetus.

Developmentally, once students reach adolescence, their focus is very self-centered. They are motivated by what's in it for them. It doesn't mean they're bad youth; their behavior is normal and developmentally appropriate.

Logical Consequences

Sometimes, young people make poor choices. When they feel threatened, bullied, disrespected, or annoyed by another youth, they may make a poor choice in how they deal with it, often acting impulsively.

Imagine the Following Scenario:

A young man hears gossip that another guy is saying bad things about his girlfriend. He announces to anyone who will listen, "I'm gonna beat that kid up! I'm gonna show him that he doesn't mess with me and my girl again." You, the teacher overhear the threat. You pull the student aside, give him time to calm down and attempt to discuss the issue.

In my experience with adolescents, talking about rules, being nice, taking the higher ground will fall on deaf ears most of the time. Lecturing the student will accomplish very little.

Taking a problem-solving approach geared towards helping the student choose a solution, while retaining his personal power, often works.

Consider the Following Script:

Teacher: "Okay, let's talk about this. Here's the problem as I understand it: Someone's talking trash about you and your girl. So what's a possible solution?"

Student: "I'm gonna beat him up!"

Teacher: Writes the solution on the top line of a T chart – one side is pros and one side is cons. Do not censor the student's words. Don't say, "Oh, you shouldn't do that," tacking on all the 'adult' reasons why it's a bad choice. Validate the student's solution by writing it down as a viable option.

Teacher: "Alright, go beat him up is your solution. What's the advantage to beating him up?"

Student: "Well, he won't mess with me again. Hell no! And I'll show him!"

Teacher: (After writing the advantage in the pro column) "Okay. So, now what are the disadvantages of beating him up?"

Student: "Well, I dunno but I've been to court once and..."

Teacher: "Yes. And do you remember the youth in the hallway that was fighting with her own best friend and accidentally broke her finger when she grabbed it during an argument. "?

Student: "Yeah."

Teacher: "She was charged in the incident by the school resource officer. She didn't mean to break her friend's finger. Even the parents of the friend didn't want to press charges, but the school resource officer had to press charges. Because it was not her first run-in with the law, she was threatened with being sent to women's prison. So, back to this chart, what's the disadvantage of beating him up?"

With almost everything presented in the media, we see fast changing scenes in short chunks of time. Consequently, our children's brains are trained and neurologically wired for rapid change stimulation (Healy, 1999).

Student: "I might end up in court, or worse, in jail."

Teacher: (After writing that consequence down) "Okay, what's another possible solution?"

Students may argue that 'taking out' someone who 'wrongs' them is the 'right,' 'good,' or 'feel good' choice and, therefore, the best choice for them. Help them to think through the long-term consequences of their actions to see that poor choices may not help them to reach the goals they have set for themselves. In addition, poor choices do not necessarily guarantee that they will not be dissed, hurt, victimized, talked trash about, etc., in the future.

The solutions must come from the student (Wubbolding, 2007). It has to be their solution (Cleary & Zimmerman, 2004). The teacher could offer a suggestion, "... maybe you walk away with your head held high." However, the teacher must not decide for the student because then the teacher owns it, not the student.

All Choices Have an Effect

There are some personality-types who aren't motivated to do work for a teacher they don't like. My son is one of them, though he has learned to compromise or he wouldn't have made it through engineering school.

I'll never forget the time when he was in his junior year in high school and working for A's so he'd be well positioned to get scholarships, he came home with a startling announcement. "Mom, I've asked to be pulled out of AP History and placed in a section with a different teacher."

Stunned, I said, "Son, you've got an A in that class. You're struggling in English. You need to keep your Grade Point Average (GPA) up. Why would you want to get out of History?"

"Because that teacher and I have a... that teacher's an idiot! I know more about history than she does," he passionately explained.

He proceeded to give me several examples of when she was incorrect in her historical facts. My son grew up reading historical novels and watching the History Channel. Honestly, he did know his history.

So, he was getting an A in the class, but he didn't like the teacher. He wanted out of that class. His reasoning was value-driven and totally illogical considering his need to keep up his GPA. Well, he wasn't allowed to get out of the class. His History teacher said there wasn't a personality conflict. His grade in that class went down quickly.

Some children don't make decisions based on logic; they make decisions based on emotional values, impulse, or simply irrational thinking (Ellis, 1999).

> *People who own their behavior and accept the consequences of their behavior learn that they have control over their destiny. They have personal power.*

We need to teach children that all choices have an effect, and that their choices could result in a positive or a negative consequence.

The Pro vs. Con Decision-Making Process:

- What are my choices?
- What are the DISADVANTAGES of each choice?
- What are the ADVANTAGES of each choice?
- Consider the options and possible consequences.
- Decide the best possible choice for YOU.

Children need to stop getting away with poor choices without experiencing consequences. I believe in logical, real-life consequences, not physical punishment, or putting them down and degrading them.

Academic Strategies that Foster Empowerment and Motivation

In a study by J. Nichols, *Empowerment and Relationships: A classroom model to enhance student motivation*, the initial findings indicate that a classroom environment which is based on positive social relationships, while encouraging student empowerment, may be the first step towards improving student motivation and achievement. She describes a classroom environment that not only attends to the social and emotional needs of students, but also to learner-centered teaching as a critical factor (Nichols, 2006).

Differentiated instruction is learner centered instruction that honors how students learn, utilizes teaching models that increase student engagement and thereby increases motivation and success.

Following, are some simple, effective, easy-to-implement strategies for engaging learners and differentiating instruction.

Focus Tools

You've got a student who cannot sit still, who
cannot cope, who's chewing
on their pen, who's fiddling
around with anything she can
get her hands on. If you try to
control her behavior, she may
settle down for a few minutes
but, in a short time, she'll be
fidgeting again.

Solution: Provide focus tools in the classroom;
quiet focus tools.

> *For more information and free
> downloads on Helping Students
> Focus, go to
> motivate.susanfitzell.com*

Cue Cards

Quietly cue children to redirect behavior or
discreetly provide positive reinforcement. Rather
than tell children, especially children on the
autistic spectrum, "Open your book. Take out
your pencil. Raise your hand." Print out a
behavior-management cue card.

When necessary to redirect a student, show the
student the card and point to the appropriate cue.
Make eye-contact with the student, smile, turn
and leave. Resist the urge to give an off-task

student a dirty look! The goal is to avoid a power struggle and help the student get back on track without humiliation.

Let's say a student is doing exceptionally well. Possibly, he's stayed on task for 10 minutes longer than usual. Show him the cue card, point to the 'high five' picture cue, smile and walk away.

Some children are embarrassed, or worse, teased, if the teacher gives them positive praise openly in the classroom. Quiet, private communication is best.

The cue-card strategy could work at home, also. If your child tends to be explosive at perceived criticism, or frustration tends to run high over homework, use the cue card to redirect or affirm positive choices.

> *To download your printable*
> *Behavior Management Cue Cards,*
> *go to motivate.susanfitzell.com*

Transitions

Seven-Minute Homework Rule

There is no reason a student has to sit down for an hour straight to do homework. For example, set a timer for seven minutes or a time you and your child can agree is reasonable to work. When the timer rings, take a 3-5 minute break.

Stand and stretch.

Get up and dance with your child for two minutes. Okay, high school children may not dance with you, but the little ones will. Be creative. Energize the brain.

Video games or TV are not recommended; it's best that they do something physical to get their brain oxygenated and primed for learning.

Timers

Use a timer. Set a timer and chunk study time for youth, especially after school for homework.

They've been sitting at a desk and working all day. There's no right way to schedule homework.

Maybe some children don't need to do all their homework right after school. Maybe there are some children who do. It depends on the youth. Negotiate with your child about homework. Make rules together, so that he feels like he is a part of the process, and then have him own the decision. Be consistent in enforcing the plan that was agreed upon.

Using timers helps students who struggle to grasp the concept of time, to internalize a sense of time. Frequent use of timers in non-threatening situations reduces timed-test fright. For some students, a timer triggers a 'beat the clock' game that is motivating. Children are used to beating the clock. Most children play timed video and app games starting at a very young age.

Lastly, timers actually help teachers stay on track.

Academic Strategies Must Fit the Student

Teachers: Instructional activities need to fit the student. Differentiate instruction, help students learn how they learn, provide opportunities that allow students to show what they know without being hindered by a learning disability.

Remember: Students who consistently fail quickly become unmotivated students.

Parents: If your child comes home with homework that doesn't fit their learning style, supplement it. If you can work with the teacher, exchange it.

My book, Please Help Me With My Homework, teaches parents exactly how to do this. Children need to be engaged in their work.

Get the book at www.amazon.com

Music that Supports Learning and Focus

I was watching a music video that one of my younger Facebook friends had posted. I decided to time the scene changes out of curiosity. Scenes changed every three seconds. I counted:

one, two, three – change; one, two, three – different picture; one, two, three – another picture. Today's youth (and many adults) have brains trained to expect a fast pace.

Music that Supports Learning

Research indicates that certain types of music support learning. Play soft music at approximately 60 beats per minute (BPM), in the background; music without words. The music is not too fast (fast dancing music) or too slow (massage music). It's just right. Consider *Mozart for Modulation* and *Baroque for Modulation* compilation CDs by Sheila Frick, OTR. These compilations were originally formulated for children in the autistic spectrum using a research-based model. They are an excellent tool for working with children and adults experiencing difficulties with sensory modulation (Lillie, 2012). That said, the music benefits all learners.

If you try to introduce classical music, some youth may complain. They'll present a case for playing their favored music. I have had students perform very well in the classroom while listening to rock music, even though this contradicts the research. As far as I know, however, there is no research to support that practice. So, it's your call as to whether you are willing to try the experiment in your classroom.

When my son was in the eighth grade, he requested that I purchase the John Williams compilation CD for him. I didn't even know who John Williams was at the time. In case you don't know, John Williams is the composer who wrote the scores for many action movies like *Raiders of the Lost Ark, E.T.*, etc.

I asked him why he wanted the compilation set. It was quite expensive.

He just said, "Because I like his music."

So he was not going to take my advice and listen to Mozart. But he *would* listen to John Williams' movie scores! Whenever he was doing his homework, I felt like I was in a movie theater watching *E.T.* or *Raiders of the Lost Ark*.

John Williams' music worked for my son. I doubt there is research that indicates that these movie scores increase achievement. I know firsthand, however, that it supported my son's efforts and made homework less drudgery. The music was uplifting, emotional, and consequently motivating. The fact that he chose the music and was studying on his terms was empowering. He was successful.

Messy Math vs. Neat Math

From Memorization and Test Taking Strategies for the Differentiated, Inclusive and RTI Classroom (S. G. Fitzell, 2010)

Particularly in learning math, disorganized workspaces clutter up working memory because students are too busy trying to make order out of chaos to focus on the actual math problem. Helping students organize their workspace is one of the best ways we can help students with math (Levine, 2003).

Following are some simple solutions to organizing math instruction for students.

- Write down the steps to the problem before solving it.
- Avoid mental arithmetic; use a scratch pad or scrap paper.
- If students become overwhelmed by looking at the entire test page, have them use blank paper to cover up everything but the problem they are working on so they don't become stressed. When they do not have to look at everything at once, they can focus more productively.

When students are working to organize their workspace or trying to decipher their work, they are using up working memory on organization rather than the math process. These strategies allow them to focus on the math.

The following strategy allows them to focus on the math instead of using mind space organizing the numbers:

Unlined paper is the worst place to do math, especially for children with visual-spatial problems. Give them lined paper sideways and have them write the numbers in the columns.

Parents: If your child comes home with math homework and it's on unlined paper, either have them switch to lined paper turned sideways or use grid/graph paper. On my website, you will find a sheet with dark lines, print it out, and put it underneath their paper. Like in the old days, when we used to write real letters on real stationery without lines and we put dark lined paper underneath to ensure we wrote in a straight line. This is the same thing, only the lines are sideways.

To download your own printable Line Sheets, go to motivate.susanfitzell.com

Speech-to-Text – Changing the World for Students with Writing Difficulties

You may be surprised to learn that I no longer write the first draft of my books in the traditional manner. Nor do I type them in the initial stages of development. I speak my books and articles into Dragon Naturally Speaking to create the first draft.

I wrote my first book using the traditional means; I typed my thoughts. For me, it was time-intensive, grueling, and exhausting. I found that I often wrote less because the task was so tiring. When I started to use Speech-to-Text, I was energized, focused on the messages that I wanted to convey, and able to easily access my research while 'speaking' the book. I never want to go back to the old way. Editing and rewriting is still grueling for me, but I got my thoughts out first and that makes the world of difference in my ability to express my ideas.

So, considering our students and those who struggle to get their ideas out, why can't someone who hasn't been assigned a scribe in their IEP, speak their initial writing?

Dragon Dictation on Mobile Devices

I realize that the need to go from thought directly to paper may be required for your state test, so I'd never suggest that teachers do one without the other. I believe, however, that there are places where it would be beneficial, and appropriate, to allow students to get their thoughts out via speech.

Doing so frees up working memory to focus totally on the goal of the task rather than on grammar, spelling, and paragraph structure. Students speak their high-level thinking and then review the written document to focus on proofreading, editing and rewriting.

Provide Visual Cues

Cognitive Maps

Developing cognitive maps and using advanced organizers increases critical thinking skills (Barba and Merchant, L. J., 1990; Snapp and Glover, J. A., 1990). Long-term memory files information in the brain through patterns, procedures, categories, pairs and rules. A mind map uses at least three of these five ways to store information.

A classic mind map begins with a word, phrase, or idea, typically placed in the center of a sheet of paper. As the author of the mind map expands upon the word or phrase in the middle, the mind map expands to include various ideas that come to mind when considering that center prompt.

Mind maps enable the brain to categorize information. A mind map is a nonlinguistic-representation method of organizing information, which enables students to file information away in long-term memory in multiple modes or memory packets.

The concept of nonlinguistic representation is so important. It's what I told my daughter to do, it's what I told my son to do, and what I told my high school students to do, especially my freshmen. I'd say, "Draw a picture!"

A side note: Motivating students to use learning strategies that are out of the norm poses its own challenges. I had to convince my high school students that drawing pictures, singing songs, and using flashcards, or color-coding, wasn't elementary. They were skeptical. I drove two hours from my home to Dartmouth College bookstore and I bought a variety of novel study tools. I did not remove the little white stickers on the back printed 'Dartmouth College Bookstore'. I brought the mini ring-bound flash cards, colorful highlighters, and mini white boards into my classroom and I told my students, "See. This isn't babyish. They're selling this at the Dartmouth College bookstore. Dartmouth College is an Ivy League school. This is what smart college students do!"

If children think the strategies are babyish, silly, or 'goofy,' educate them about how the brain learns.

I taught mind mapping to my daughter and the technique got her through Fluids class in Engineering school. I walked into her dorm room one day and she had color-coded, mnemonic-enhanced mind maps on the wall. This technique didn't just help her in high school, it didn't just help students with special needs; this technique helped my daughter get through her college Engineering classes. She said, "Mom, this is the only way that I managed to pass Fluids." (I still have no idea what Fluids are!)

Shivahn's Mind-Map Wall

Read and Draw What You Read

If your children or students are reading, have them draw pictures while they're reading to help them remember what they've read. Or, provide more structure and have them create a storyboard or comic strip to illustrate what they have read.

For students who struggle with sequential memory: As students are reading a textbook or story, instruct them to draw pictures on adding machine tape of the important information (characters, historical figures, places, events, etc.) in the order that they appear in the information source. Walk students through the process.

A. Remind students to start at the beginning of the tape and work left to right.

B. Have models available as visual reminders for students.

To view a video about Sequencing Strips, go to motivate.susanfitzell.com

Movement or Kinesthetic Learners

Many students are bodily-kinesthetic learners. They learn through their bodies and they need to move. They fidget and squirm. The following ideas can help make movement into a positive learning force in your classroom. These tips were contributed by Fritz Bell in *Creative Classrooms* (Bell, 2005).

- Have your students act out vocabulary words with their bodies. This will give them a visual picture to remember their words.
- Have the class clap out the syllables in the names of their classmates or their vocabulary words. This is a great strategy for helping kids remember long, multisyllabic words.
- Kinesthetic alphabetizing: Put vocabulary words on individual cards and pass them out to the class. Then have them move around the room and, at a signal from you, form groups of five or less (depending on grade level and vocabulary) and line up in alphabetical order based on the words on their cards.
- Kinesthetic prepositions: Have students use an object such as a pencil and hold it in, under, over, next to, beside, or above their desks to act out prepositions.

Movement wakes up the brain. I used to take my son outside and we'd play basketball while doing spelling words. Shoot the ball, spell a word. Shoot the ball, spell a word.

Memorization Strategies

The following is adapted from Memorization and Test-Taking Strategies (S. G. Fitzell, 2010)

I use color categorizing for grouping letters into meaningful chunks to help improve children's retention in working memory. Parents, teachers, anybody can add this to an assignment. Youth can learn to color code for themselves.

Using memory strategies doesn't need to be assigned by a teacher and it doesn't interfere with anything a teacher might be assigning. Therefore, if you are a parent and you believe that your child would benefit from memory strategies, supplement their home study with those strategies, regardless of what the teacher assigns.

Many students with learning disabilities struggle with memory deficits. Primarily, they forget information they need to do well on tests or to do the higher-level thinking required for problem solving, analysis and synthesis. For example, if students can't remember basic math facts, even if they have a calculator at their disposal, they will take longer to complete a test, thereby impacting their test scores.

Working memory space for these students is being used up with basic calculations rather than higher-level thinking skills (Levine, 2003). Students who struggle to remember the details of a story can't draw inferences from those details because they can't remember the sequence of events or what happened at various parts of the story.

Remembering the details of what is being taught is critical to comprehending, applying and analyzing the course material. An intervention strategy to differentiate instruction for students struggling to remember information in the classroom is to teach short-term memory strategies.

Limit Information

The brain can only hold seven pieces of information at a time in short-term memory. What this means is that if we teach for 20 minutes and we've given students more than seven things to remember, it's too much. If we put up a slide and there are more than seven things on it, it's probably too much for the brain. The only way we can sometimes get away with more than seven facts is if they are written in a very large font, or if we 'chunk' related information by color. The brain can process information quickly off an overhead or from a PowerPoint presentation if we've chunked it with color. So, if we have eight or nine things, we might be able to use color to make it more like seven if some of those things go together.

For example, five facts about short-term memory might be green, five facts about working memory could be brown, and five facts about long-term memory could be black. We chunk related information by color.

Paraphrase Immediately

Another strategy to enhance short-term memory so information isn't 'gone' in two seconds is to have a student paraphrase what we just taught. For example, after you've taught something important, ask a volunteer to paraphrase that information for the class. Most likely, your students will not relate the information in the same words you used, which will be novel to the brain. This strategy only takes seconds to do, yet it lets your students hear the information again, in a different way, with a different voice. The brain likes novelty and will remember the information better.

Paraphrase One Hour Later

Ask your students to paraphrase information that was shared earlier in the day. When they take something you taught an hour ago and bring it back into play, it returns to short-term memory and is then pushed into working memory. Using this paraphrasing strategy in your classrooms will help students to remember what you are teaching.

Snapshot Devices

Another way to present information visually is to use a snapshot device. Snapshot devices take the concepts we've already talked about to another level because their purpose is to take a 'snapshot' of information and represent it visually so students will remember it. For instance, you've taught about how the West was settled and explained that certain inventions were involved, such as the six-shooter, the windmill, the sod house, the locomotive, and barbed wire. Your class creates a picture that includes all those items.

A snapshot device is a picture with all of the things you've taught in it. However, it's a scene,

not just a collection of individual pictures. If you just draw pictures of a six-shooter, a windmill, and a sod house, with no way to relate these things to each other, you are drawing 'unconnected' images. Snapshot devices can also illustrate more complex concepts like diffusion of molecules. In the following example, analogy was combined with text and a snapshot device to provide a powerful visual.

With a snapshot device, you take the information and make it into a scene to think about. Students will remember the cowboy with the six-shooters and the train coming down the hill behind the sod house. They will see the scene in their minds' eye.

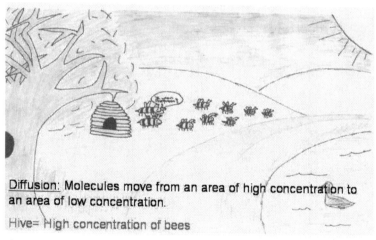

Diffusion: Molecules move from an area of high concentration to an area of low concentration.

Hive= High concentration of bees

Surrounding area = Low concentration of bees

Contributed by 7th Grade Science Class, Kennedy Middle School, Waltham, MA

Visual Homework

Having your students draw a snapshot device is a much more meaningful homework assignment than filling in a worksheet. You might also draw a scene that includes some of the facts that you want students to remember for the topic or unit you are teaching and let them add to it and color it. Sometimes, the best homework we can give students is the kind that utilizes proven memory strategies.

Create Acrostics and Mnemonics

Mnemonic devices are a type of linguistic memory strategy. Using a word or sentence to represent a list of things or a series of information that you want students to remember is an age-old concept. For instance, the term LASER

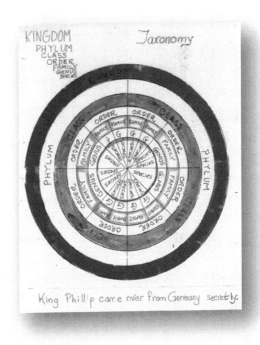

means 'Light Amplification by Stimulated Emission of Radiation.' Use a word to represent information where each letter of that word stands for something.

Another type of mnemonic is an acrostic: A sentence where each word represents part of the information to be remembered. In the example below, our high school Science class was learning taxonomy. A common acrostic for this concept is 'King Philip came over from Germany secretly.' We wrote out the sentence, and then we created a visual that illustrates the concept. The verbal information, supported by the visual image, incorporates a number of brain-based memory principles.

Mnemonic Homework

There are always lists and bits of information that we want students to know and remember. What if we take that information – English vocabulary; social studies' dates, names, or famous people; science terms; or any other subject, such as art or music – and have them make mnemonics with that information?

Have your students design their own mnemonic devices for homework. Have the class vote on the best choices and publish them for everyone to use. These powerful strategies help students remember information. We need to teach these strategies and encourage students to use them.

Chunking Information

The brain can only hold seven chunks of information in short-term memory at a time. Think about how we naturally work with information that we can break up, or chunk, into parts.

Three Card Match – A Review Strategy

Flash cards for studying have been around since before I was in school. We can take the flash card concept to another level when working with vocabulary and other concepts by adding definitions or descriptors to our terms and visual clues. Three Card Match is a memory game that puts the concepts of print, color, and visuals together using vocabulary, definitions, or mnemonics along with visual clues.

One year, I had a group of students who were in a general education classroom for the very first time. We were doing inclusion in a class of 27 students, 13 of who were on an IEP, with only two receiving modified tests. They had to learn 20 constellation names, the unique features of those constellations and what the constellation looked like as part of the curriculum.

These students with special needs had never been required to memorize anything so complex in their self-contained classrooms. I truly did not believe they were capable of memorizing that much information. I was 'raised' as a teacher in an age where we learned that if something was difficult for students, we'd find a work-around rather than require students to do a task that fell into the realm of their disability.

Since this memorization task was part of the general curriculum standards, we had to find a way to help the students be successful. We used Three Card Match to assist students in the process of learning and remembering the constellation information. Every student passed their test. I was humbled. I really didn't believe, at the onset, that the students on my caseload and in this inclusion class were capable of succeeding with the assignment.

Use Three Card Match any time you have terms or items you need students to remember. If you've got a ready-made matching test, cut it up so there's a word and a matching statement that goes with the word. Then add a memory cue: a picture, a diagram, or a personal experience, and you've got your Three Card Match. The third card is typically something that helps students remember.

To view a video on Three Card Match, go to motivate.susanfitzell.com

Remember, research indicates that we learn the most when we teach others. When two people work together to study, they are teaching each other.

Technology: Motivating and Engaging

Simple Ideas for Introducing Technology into the Classroom

Technology is not meant to be cumbersome, nor should it be looked at as an add-on or substitution for a regular lesson plan. With a few easy-to-use tools and apps, classroom instruction can be enhanced to be more inclusive of different learning styles and abilities, to better engage students in course material, and to meet students in the digital world they so enjoy. Below are some ideas for using technology in the classroom that range from short, simple techniques, to more sophisticated ideas that are more interactive and even student-led.

Use of Videos to Enhance Understanding, Connection and Learning

Videos can be used effectively to bring material alive and help students connect on more than one level. Short, targeted clips can be more effective than long films, in that they can help break up longer lessons or difficult material.

Free educational clips are available from sources like LearnOutLoud, Google Videos, or the Khan Academy – one of the most comprehensive sources for free educational material on the internet for math.

iTunes University (iTunesU) is a goldmine of college coursework, flipped lesson plans, entire teachable units aligned to standards, audio books and more. Parents exclaim, "I don't know how to help my child with his homework!" iTunes University has all kinds of courses that you can use to have children do supplemental homework, or for supplemental reinforcement.

Also, products like DamnVid make downloading and converting videos easy for teachers, while VLC Media Player is a free video + player that will rarely show an error message. It plays just about everything!

Free Online Tech Resources

Some technology can actually help save money while providing students with an impressive array of resources. Project Gutenberg is a free online resource that offers the full text of books in the public domain. Most classics fall under this category. Students can read classics online, or teachers can source pieces of different texts for comparative purposes. LibriVox is a similar source, and the books are in audio-book form. This can allow students who are not strong readers to benefit from the material, despite their reading disability. This is not meant to replace reading practice, but can help get struggling or reluctant readers interested in books and help them keep up with a pace of reading that might otherwise be unattainable for them.

The Lesser-Known Gem: Public Libraries

For more recent books, many libraries offer an extensive range of new releases in e-book format, which can be read on e-readers, smartphones, tablets, or PCs at no charge. Many school libraries simply can't compete with the titles available through these online sources, and students can borrow titles any time day or night, without the need to physically go to a library. For students without libraries at school or in their neighborhood, online borrowing can be an excellent option.

Technology and Student Skill Development

Technology can also help students gain valuable skills needed to succeed in their subjects, such as effective note-taking skills and being able to effectively organize, prioritize, and sort information. Online note-taking programs, mind-mapping, or brainstorming apps can help students take notes and organize information in ways that make the most sense for them.

In class, brainstorming or mind-mapping apps can be used as guides for students to organize information in a way that is helpful for visual learners as well.

Voice-to-Text as a Solution for Struggling Writers

For students who are slow writers, voice-to-text apps can help students with processing difficulties take notes from readings in a way that works best for them. Dictation into voice-to-text programs is a common practice used by business professionals and others, so it is a valuable skill for any student to learn. Voice-to-text programs are wonderful for use in language learning classrooms, as well. They help students practice enunciating words clearly, so that the application can understand what they are trying to say. Students could practice just free speaking into the program, or can work on certain sounds, words, or phrases that may be giving them trouble.

Note-Taking Apps with Time-Stamp Recording Capability

There's an app, AudioNote, which is fantastic because it audiotapes the instructor while you're typing. Then you just click what you've typed and it repeats what the instructor said.
This is very useful if you're doing notes with your child, or you're talking a student through a

problem, as you can use AudioNote to tape what you're saying to your student or child, and then they can play it back with the typed or illustrated instructions. You might draw pictures when it's playing back or you can record while drawing pictures and verbalizing the information labeled in the picture. It's fantastic.

Portable App Drawing Programs (PC Based)

RealWorld Paint is a free, feature-rich, but easy-to-use paint program for creating or enhancing visuals that students can work with in the classroom. Use it to visually capture notes or to categorize homework with color. It's easy to use and makes learning fun.

The Power of Songs for Memorization

No matter what subject you teach, using singing and music to help students remember material can be one of the most powerful tools in your teaching toolkit. Math teachers use 'Pop! Goes the Weasel' to help students remember the quadratic formula. English teachers use 'Mary Had a Little Lamb' to teach the various forms of 'to be.' And in Social Studies... well, let's look at an example.

I was recently talking about memorization with my Kung Fu teacher, who's a few years younger than me, and he had a great story about using music as a memory strategy. When he was in high school, he had a tough assignment – to memorize the Constitution. He studied it every night, but just couldn't seem to get it into his head.

One day, he was talking about this assignment at lunch when a girl jumped in and asked him if he'd tried using the song. It turned out that she'd seen Schoolhouse Rock on a Saturday morning cartoon, and the show had a song for the Constitution. Soon, word got out to all the students in the class about the song from Schoolhouse Rock – and all of the students passed the assignment.

The teacher was flabbergasted – he'd never seen a class where every student was able to memorize the Constitution. The funniest thing to me was when my Kung Fu teacher started singing the song on the spot; 20 years later, he still remembered it. Talk about learning!

As teachers, we absolutely must use every tool we have available to us, and music is one of the most powerful strategies we can utilize. You don't have to be a Broadway star to help your students use music and singing in the classroom. Whether you teach them a song for the multiplication tables or have them make up lyrics for karaoke that are relevant to your unit, by attaching something new to something the students already know, they'll learn.

Turn the page for a preview of Susan Fitzell's groundbreaking book on bullying prevention: *Free The Children: Conflict Education for Strong, Peaceful Minds* Available at Amazon.com in paperback or Kindle

What right do I have to teach children to be empowered?

An excerpt from Free the Children: Conflict Education for Strong, Peaceful Minds (S. Fitzell, 1997)

No matter what you do to try to reach them, some children pull away and withdraw. Why?

I looked into his tear-brimmed eyes as he fought for composure, and my heart broke for his pain. Never, when I started this conflict education work, did I expect to meet such strong emotion and resistance from a child. I might have expected some avoidance from students who exhibited a great deal of bullying behaviors. I did not expect it from this child.

At the beginning of the school year, this child blended in with all the other faces that I was working to come to know. He seemed like every other kid. Then, as the weeks went on and my lessons spoke more of how to be empowered and of how not to be a victim, he withdrew further and further into his shell. He'd sit in the back. His body language screamed with resentment and non-compliance to my requests for participation. He had the look of a hardened young man while he was just a young boy. I wondered how I could reach him. What was going on inside him? He told me he hated my lessons. I wondered why.

One day, I spoke with the classroom teacher about my concerns. I asked her what I needed to do to reach this child. I was only in the classroom once a week for my lesson. She knew this child and how to approach him. Sighing, she shook her head with concern. She had recently found out that he was being bullied at home by his older brothers. Steps were being taken to improve his situation. That day she asked me to discuss with the class what they should do if they are bullied at home. Whom should the children talk to? I spent time discussing options with the children. When everyone seemed ready to move on, I continued with my lesson.

For the next few weeks, things seemed to improve for this child. The classroom teacher praised him for his positive attitude and his progress. Over a period of a couple of months, I saw him go from wearing a hunted, stone-faced look to being a relaxed, happy child... to being a defeated, teary-eyed boy.

It was one of my last sessions with the class. I wanted everyone in the group to participate in an assertive skill technique. This technique was to be used when two children were playing together and one child got too rough. The 'victim' would swing his/her arms to break the hold of the 'bully,' look the 'bully' in the eyes, and say loudly and clearly, "Let go! Don't ever do that again! Give me some space." This child physically moved away from the activity. He looked panicked and threatened. I tried to encourage him to participate, and he halfheartedly swung his arms, only to be greeted by laughter from some of the other children. His eyes filled with tears. He worked hard not to let them flow.

I felt at a loss. This child, more than any other child in the classroom, needed these skills desperately. The teacher strongly reprimanded the other kids for laughing, believing that the laughter had upset the boy. My sense of the situation was that this child felt defeated. He did not believe that he could succeed in defending himself. He did not even want to try. I felt that he resented me for telling him that the skills that I taught could help him. I did not understand him. What did I really know about his situation?

Everything that I tried to teach him was in direct conflict with verbal and non-verbal messages he was getting at home. He is outnumbered at home. He is a victim, trapped. How dare I tell him to live differently?

All my lessons seemed to do was bring up powerful feelings of hopelessness and futility. Having to stand up and participate in the activity seemed to threaten him so terribly that he used all his energy to divert his attention elsewhere and to exclude himself. To do the role-playing, he had to confront his emotions – something he was not ready to do.

When I reflect upon this situation, many conflicting thoughts go through my mind. What right do I have to teach children how to be empowered, if empowerment is not valued at home? Am I setting some kids up for a bigger fall if they try these skills in a situation where they are truly powerless? In The Dance of Anger, Harriet Goldhor Learner writes about 'Change Back!' reactions from others.

In a family, each member comes to play a role. Our place in the family is to keep that role so as not to rock the boat. When one person in the family attempts to change his/her role and to think and act differently, other family members often react with strong resistance. That resistance may cause the one who wants to change to retreat back into old patterns. A young child could not possibly withstand this resistance and pressure without adult support. The 'Change Back!' reactions of other family members could leave a child feeling totally defeated.

I counter these thoughts with the belief that what I am doing is helping the greater majority of kids. Most will feel more empowered and confident to defend themselves, more self-aware and able to adjust their reactions and responses in conflict situations in order to diffuse tension. Most children will use these skills effectively. Most will become more aware of the influence the media and environment have on their attitudes and reactions.

I couldn't possibly give up what I do because I believe in it passionately. However, I will now be much more sensitive to the resistant child who surfaces in my lessons. I will work to know that child, to know the obstacles he/she faces, and to adapt what I teach so that I don't set this child up for failure. Maybe what I do will help; maybe it won't. When I falter and ask myself whether it is worth it, I have to know that I couldn't live with myself if I didn't try.

What right do I have to teach children how to be empowered, if empowerment is not valued at home?

Am I setting some kids up for a bigger fall if they try these skills in a situation where they are truly powerless?

Get your own copy of Free the Children: Conflict Education for Strong, Peaceful Minds at

www.amazon.com

Susan Offers Professional Programs Customized to Your Needs

As a seasoned educator, Susan's straight-forward, common-sense approach and her practical, research-based strategies yield positive, measurable results; whether she's presenting a one-day program or facilitating long-term consulting. All programs can be customized to meet Common Core State Standards (CCSS) and Next Generation State Standards (NGSS). Please contact us today and let us put the right pieces into a program for you. Below is a partial list of training programs, for a complete list look at Hire Susan on susanfitzell.com.

For TEACHERS

Co-teaching and Collaboration

Learn realistic methods for taking co-teaching up a level through data-driven grouping strategies, station teaching and efficient time management.

Differentiated Instruction and Special Needs

Discover ways that the brain learns and discuss a variety of brain-based, research supported, "implement tomorrow" strategies that will help teachers reach ALL the learners in their classrooms.

Memorization & Test Mastery

Realistic strategies to foster memory in the classroom for all learners and to bypass memory difficulties for under-performing students.

Paraprofessionals

Develop an understanding of the potential benefits of collaboration and define approaches to achieving those benefits.

Response to Intervention (or Really Terrific Instruction)

Practical, classroom-tested techniques as well as user-friendly materials that can be implemented immediately in your classroom.

iPad and Mobile Technology

Discover practical ways to use technology to accelerate and differentiate.

For ADMINISTRATORS

Coaching Teachers to Excellence!

How does an administrator lead teachers to implement exemplary teaching and learning practices? What approach motivates and inspires rather than instills fear, resentment and resistance?

Classroom Walkthroughs

What should I see when I walk through an inclusive, differentiated classroom? Administrators have a key role in ensuring that students' learning needs are met. In this dynamic, practical session, you will learn what best-practice, researched based strategies and methods might be used to engage all learners so that students improve test scores and reach their potential.

Co-Teaching for Administrators: Who, What, When, Why & How

Co-teaching is an option for inclusive schools that can yield positive results IF implemented with fidelity. The role of administration is critical in ensuring that co-teaching works to benefit teachers and students. Learn what does an administrator needs to know about co-teaching.

Solution-based, Best-Practice Coaching

Susan Fitzell works with administrators, general and special education teachers, and paraprofessionals to implement strategies in the classroom that respond to student needs and support an environment that increases achievement.

For PARENTS & STUDENTS

Increase Student Success by Building Vocabulary with Fun, Effective Strategies

How to help youth build better vocabularies using fun, effective strategies and tools.

Please Help Me With My Homework! A Parent and Child Strategy Workshop

Help children finish homework assignments successfully!

Techno-Strategy Blast!

Whether students are gifted, struggling learners, or have special needs, participants will leave this workshop with technology-centered strategies to differentiate instruction.

For More Information:

e-Mail Susan at sfitzell@susanfitzell.com or visit **susanfitzell.com**

What people say about Susan:

"Susan's expertise and instructional support helped promote a school-wide belief that all students can be successful learners. It was through her guidance that we were able to make AYP and be removed from the list of schools 'in need of improvement.'"

Dr. Frank L. Mellaci, Vice-Principal
White Mountains Regional High School

"From the time I walked into the room, I was intrigued. Your presentation style and electric personality captivates the audience - small or large, and empowers each workshop participant to become the best educator s/he can."

Joy L.Tibbott
Director of Special Education
Northern Cambria School District

"Susan has a strong and positive ability to relate to teachers and to support and guide them with focused feedback as she becomes a member of the school's instructional team. Susan is very good at assessing exactly what needs to be done within the school and providing focused and prioritized strategies for school-based and district-level administrators as a part of the school improvement process."

Brent Williams, Principal
North Lenoir High School

"Her keynote was fantastic. What I really liked was she brought out, for our parents and educators, contributions that famous people with disabilities have made, and actually woven in people with Down syndrome, as well as one of our fellow speakers, so she was really great. I've heard lots of comments from her *other sessions that the information she gave them includes techniques they can take back with them and actually utilize in their classrooms right away."*

Maureen Tignor,
Dallas Down Syndrome Guild

"It is truly hard to find a presenter with the level of expertise to empower change as Susan did for our districts."

Ginny Phegley
Greene & Sullivan
Special Education Cooperative

Please Leave a Review!

We need your feedback to help with our non-stop efforts to provide you with the best information possible. Please take a few minutes to leave an honest review of this book by following these easy steps:

1. Go to **amazon.com**

2. Search for the book you wish to review by typing the title of this book in the search box at the top of the page.

3. Click on the image of this book you on the search results page.

5. Just below the book title and author's name, there is a link to the reviews that have already been left, if any, or the link to leave a review. Click on the link.

6. At the top of the page that opens, click on the "Create Your Own Review" button.

7. Follow the prompts to leave your own review of the book.

Thank you!

Bibliography

Barba and Merchant, L. J., R. H. (1990). The Effects of Embedding Generative Cognitive Strategies in Science Software. *Journal of Computers in Mathematics and Science Teaching, 10*(1), 59–65.

Bell, F. (2005). *Total Body Learning: Movement and Academics* (p. 58). Manchester: Cogent Catalyst Publications.

Bénabou, R., & Tirole, J. (2003). Intrinsic and Extrinsic Motivation. *Review of Economic Studies, 70*(3), 489–520. doi:10.1111/1467-937x.00253

Bluestein, J. E. (2008). *The Win-Win Classroom: A Fresh and Positive Look at Classroom Management* (pp. 55–70). Thousand Oaks, CA: Corwin Press.

Brooks, C. F., & Young, S. L. (2011). Are Choice-Making Opportunities Needed in the Classroom? Using Self- Determination Theory to Consider Student Motivation and Learner Empowerment. *International Journal of Teaching & Learning in Higher Education, 23*(1), 48–59.

Cleary, T. J., & Zimmerman, B. J. (2004). Self-regulation empowerment program: A school-based program to enhance self-regulated and self-motivated cycles of student learning.

Psychology in the Schools, 41(5), 537–550.
doi:10.1002/pits.10177

Ellis, A. (1999). *How to Make Yourself Happy
and Remarkably Less Distrubable* (p. 224).
atascadero, CA: Impact Publishers, Inc.

Ellis, A. (2007). *Overcoming Resistance: A
Rational Emotive Behavior Therapy Integrated
Approach* (2nd ed., pp. 44–45). New York,
N.Y.: Springer Publishing Company.

Fitzell, S. (2010). *Paraprofessionals and Teachers
Working Together: Highly Effective
Strategies for Inclusive Classroom* (p. 151).
Cogent Catalyst Publications.

Fitzell, S. G. (2007). *Transforming Anger to
Personal Power: An Anger Management
Curriculum for Grades 6-12* (p. 125).
Champaign, IL: Research Press.

Fitzell, S. G. (2010). *Memorization and Test
Taking Strategies for the Differentiated,
Inclusive and RTI Classroom* (1st ed., p.
111). Manchester: Cogent Catalyst
Publications.

Flowerday, T., & Schraw, G. (2000). Teacher
beliefs about instructional choice: A
phenomenological study. *Journal of
Educational Psychology, 92*(4), 634–645.
doi:10.1037//0022-0663.92.4.634

Gordon, R. G. and M. (2006). *The Turned-off
Child: Learned Helplessness and School*

Failure (p. 324). Salt Lake City, UT: Millennial Mind Publishing.

Healy, J. M. (1999). *Endangered Minds: Why Children Dont Think And What We Can Do About It* (2nd ed., p. 392). New York, N.Y.: Simon & Schuster.

Hong, Z. R., Lin, H.-S., & Lawrenz, F. P. (2012). Effects of an Integrated Science and Societal Implication Intervention on Promoting Adolescents' Positive Thinking and Emotional Perceptions in Learning Science. *International Journal of Science Education*. doi:10.1080/09500693.2011.623727

Jansen, A. S., Nguyen, X. V, Karpitskiy, V., Mettenleiter, T. C., & Loewy, A. D. (1995). Central command neurons of the sympathetic nervous system: basis of the fight-or-flight response. *Science (New York, N.Y.)*, *270*(5236), 644–646. doi:10.1126/science.270.5236.644

Kohn, A. (1993). Choices for Children: Why and How to Let Students Decide. *Phi Delta Kappan*, *75*(1), 8–16,18–21 Sep 1993.

Levine, M. (2003). *A Mind At A Time* (p. 352). New York, NY: Simon and Schuster.

Lillie, S. M. (2012). *The Effect of Rythm and Melody on Language Development and Sensory Organization in Children with Autism*. University of Northern Colorado.

Mikulincer, M. (1995). Human Learned Helplessness: A Coping Perspective. In C. R. Snyder (Ed.), *The Springer Series in Social Clinical Psychology* (pp. 263–267). Lawrence, Kansas: Springer Publishing Company.

Miller, W. R., & Seligman, M. E. (1975). Depression and learned helplessness in man. *Journal of Abnormal Psychology, 84*(3), 228–238. doi:10.1037/h0076720

Nichols, J. D. (2006). Empowerment and relationships: A classroom model to enhance student motivation. *Learning Environments Research, 9*(2), 149–161. doi:10.1007/s10984-006-9006-8

Oei, N. Y. L., Everaerd, W. T. A. M., Elzinga, B. M., van Well, S., & Bermond, B. (2006). Psychosocial stress impairs working memory at high loads: an association with cortisol levels and memory retrieval. *Stress (Amsterdam, Netherlands), 9*(3), 133–141. doi:10.1080/10253890600965773

Peterson, C., Maier, S. F., & Seligman, M. E. P. (1993). *Learned helplessness: A theory for the age of personal control. Learned helplessness: A theory for the age of personal control.* (pp. 359–xi, 359). Oxford University Press, New York, NY. doi:10.1097/00008877-199204001-00099

Shohamy, D., & Adcock, R. A. (2010). Dopamine and adaptive memory. *Trends in Cognitive Sciences, 14*(10), 464–472. doi:10.1016/j.tics.2010.08.002

Simmons, A. M., & Page, M. (2010). Motivating Students through Power and Choice. *English Journal, 100*(1), 65–69.

Simon, M. A. (1995). The unspoken language of motivation. *Scholastic Coach and Athletic Director, 64*(6), 68.

Snapp and Glover, J. A., J. C. (1990). Advance Organizers and Study Questions. *Journal of Educational Research, 83*(5), 266–271.

Wubbolding, R. E. (2007). Glasser Quality School. *Group Dynamics: Theory, Research, and Practice.* doi:10.1037/1089-2699.11.4.253

37307579R00077

Made in the USA
Middletown, DE
26 February 2019